THE BRAIN
AND
NERVOUS SYSTEM

Steve Parker

Series Consultant

Dr Alan Maryon-Davis

MB, BChir, MSc, MRCP, FFCM

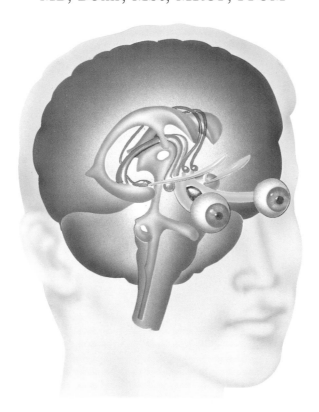

Franklin Watts

London • New York • Toronto • Sydney

Words in bold appear in the glossary.

© 1989 Franklin Watts

Original edition first published in 1981

Franklin Watts
96 Leonard Street
London
EC2A 4RH

Published in the United States by
Franklin Watts Inc.
387 Park Avenue South
New York, NY 10016

Published in Australia by
Franklin Watts Australia
14 Mars Road
Lane Cove
NSW 2066

ISBN: 0 86313 865 9

Illustrations: Andrew Aloof, Bob Chapman, Howard Dyke,
Hayward Art Group, David Holmes, Abdul Aziz Khan, David
Mallot.

Photographs: Allsport 5, 15, 41; Steve Benbow 27; Tim Betts 24;
Anthony Browne from Alice's Adventures in Wonderland by
Lewis Carroll illustrated by Anthony Browne, published by Julia
MacRae Books 26; Chapel Studios 36; Chris Fairclough 17, 37;
Network/Anthea Sieveking 31; Science Photo Library front cover,
7, 9t, 9b, 18, 21, 23, 42; Watney 4; ZEFA 6, 45.

Printed in Belgium

Contents

Introduction

It fits snugly inside the skull, taking up the top half of the head. It weighs about 1.25 kilograms and has the appearance of whitish-pink blancmange. Inside, it has a system of fluid-filled channels and cavities. Its upper curved surface has a pattern of bulges and grooves – like a huge, wrinkled walnut. It is the human **brain**.

The brain is the control centre of the body. It is involved in almost everything you do, including body movement – from turning a somersault to scanning this page with your eyes. It is also the site of unseen mental processes, such as thoughts and feelings, memories, emotions and learning.

The brain is the centre of the body's nervous system. Like other body parts, it is made of microscopic building-blocks called cells. The characteristic types of cells in the brain are **nerve** cells, or **neurons** (page 18). Also made of nerve cells, and joined to the bottom of the brain like a long stalk, is the **spinal cord**.

Millions of other nerve cells spread through the body, joining the brain and spinal cord to the various parts and organs. Batches of these nerve cells are grouped together, like the many wires in a telephone cable, to form the body's nerves. The nerves look more like lengths of string than miniature electrical cables.

The brain and spinal cord are together called the **central nervous system**. The nerves that run to other organs, such as the eyes, ears, arms and feet, are called the **peripheral nervous system**.

Bigger means cleverer?

- There is no simple, direct link between brain size and intelligence. What seems more important is brain size compared to body size, and how the brain is constructed.
- The sperm whale has the biggest brain, weighing up to 9 kg. This is about 0.02% of its body weight.
- An elephant's brain, at 5 kg, is 0.1% of its body weight.
- A human brain is around 2% of the body weight.

▷ Faces in the crowd. Inside each head, a brain is deep in concentration.

▽ A side view of the human brain, the control centre of the body.

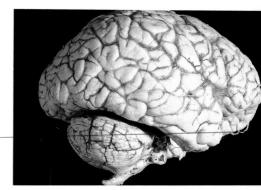

Protecting the brain

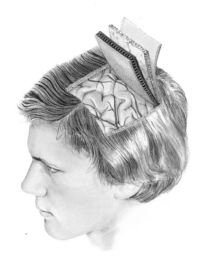

△ This "peeled-away" view shows the various layers covering and protecting the brain, including the skin, skull bone and three meninges.

Because the brain and spinal cord are so vitally important to the body, they need to be well protected from knocks and other physical harm.

Both parts are shielded by hard, tough bone. The top part of the skull, the cranium, surrounds the brain and forms a rigid "brainbox" to prevent it being crushed. Although the skull bone is not particularly thick, its rounded design gives great strength, like an egg-shell. The cranium is covered by the skin of the scalp, and also in most people by hair, which gives added protection.

The spinal cord runs down inside the neck and back, so it is shielded by other body parts such as muscles. In addition, it is protected by the linked bones of the spine. Each spinal bone (vertebra) has a hole through it, and the holes of all the bones line up to create a tunnel which houses the spinal cord (and some main nerves). This design

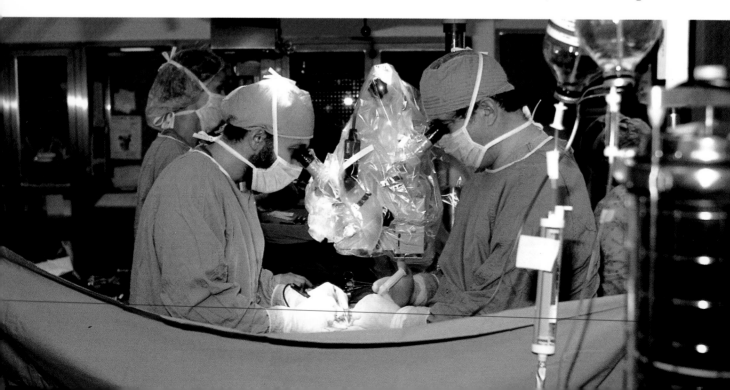

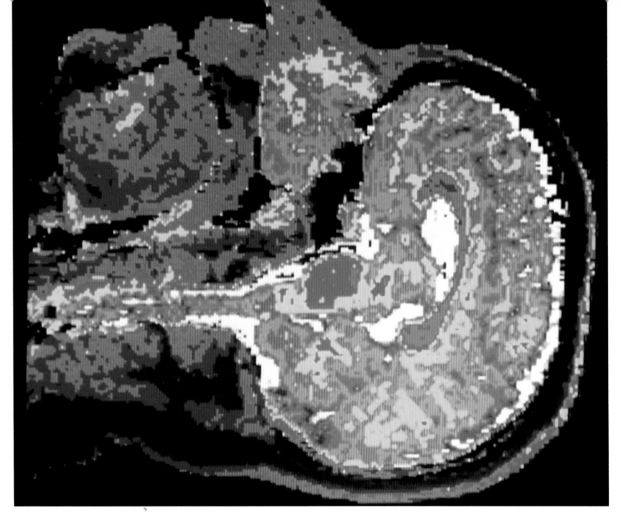

△ A living brain inside its owner's head is revealed by **NMR (nuclear magnetic resonance) scanning**. The **cerebrospinal fluid**, which surrounds and cushions the brain and spinal cord, shows up as white.

◁ The neurosurgeon is a specialist on operations involving the brain and nerves. He or she uses laser-powered scalpels, operating microscopes and many other technological aids to perform operations such as brain tumour removal.

provides protection for the spinal cord, yet also allows flexibility, so that the spine can bend and twist without kinking or knotting the spinal cord.

A sudden knock on the head could shake the brain within the hard, rigid skull, and bruise it. This is made less likely by three layers of **membranes**, the **meninges**, which cover the brain and cushion it from shocks, knocks and vibrations from outside.

The outer of the three meninges is the dura mater. It is tough and leathery, and gives good support. The middle layer is the arachnoid, a spongy substance. Inside this is a fluid-filled space that provides cushioning. The inner layer is the pia mater, which is much thinner and closely follows the bumps and wrinkles on the brain's surface.

The spinal cord

The spinal cord is a long "bundle" of nerves, extending from the base of the brain. It is so called because it runs along the inside of the spine (backbone). It acts as the main link between the body and the brain.

The upper end of the spinal cord merges with the base of the brain, in the middle of the head, at about the level of the bottom of the ears. The lower end is around two-thirds of the way down the spine. Below this, the spinal cord itself splits to form several main nerves that continue within the spine, eventually running to the legs and feet.

If you could cut through the spinal cord, you would see a greyish H-shape along its middle, surrounded by a whiter substance. The H is known as the **grey matter**, and it consists of thousands of the central parts or "bodies" of the nerve cells (page 18). The **white matter** around the H is made mainly of the long, thin, wire-like extensions of the nerve cells, called **axons**.

The spinal cord is almost totally encased by the spinal bones. Yet nerves running to and from other parts of the body must somehow connect to it, in order to relay nerve messages between body and brain. These nerves branch off the spinal cord at regular intervals and pass through the narrow gaps between the spinal bones. In total, 31 pairs of spinal nerves branch from the cord.

Some parts of the nerves bring information to the spinal cord, to be passed up to the brain. These include nerve messages from the skin, about touch, temperature and pain; and messages from the internal organs and the muscles of the limbs. Nerves that carry incoming information are called sensory nerves.

Other nerves are motor nerves. They carry outgoing information – signals from the brain, which travel down the spinal cord to the various parts. These motor messages activate muscles and so control the movements of body and limbs.

Like the brain, the spinal cord is wrapped in the three layers of the meninges. It is also cushioned from knocks by the fluid between the arachnoid and pia mater layers. Sometimes, germs get into the meninges and fluid, and they may multiply causing an infection. This is called **meningitis**. In some cases the swollen, inflamed meninges may press on the brain or spinal cord and cause damage, even threatening life.

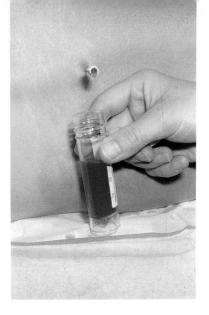

△ The cerebrospinal fluid around the spinal cord can be sampled by the technique of lumbar puncture. A hypodermic needle is inserted through the back muscles and between the spinal bones, and a small amount of fluid is collected. It is normally almost clear. In this case it is bloodstained because of bleeding within the skull.

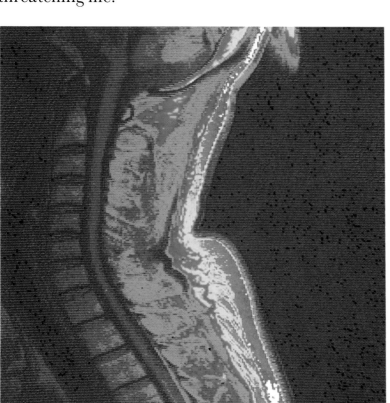

◁ This NMR scan of the neck reveals the spinal cord as a thin blue line running down inside the spinal bones, which show up to its left as squarish blocks. To the far left is the darker blue tube of the windpipe. On the right are the muscles of the neck (brighter blue), and the fat and skin on the back of the neck (red and yellow).

Inside the brain

The brain is not one large lump of tangled nerve cells. It is highly organized and has several main parts, as well as many smaller, less obvious ones.

The most obvious parts of the brain are the two large, wrinkled lobes which extend around the top and sides. They are the **cerebral hemispheres**, which together form the **cerebrum** (page 16). Below the cerebrum, at the back of the brain, is a smaller wrinkled lobe, the **cerebellum** (page 14).

Below the cerebrum, in front of the cerebellum, is the **brain stem** (page 12), which merges into the top of the spinal cord. Several smaller parts are situated just in front of the brain stem, including the **hypothalamus** and the pituitary gland (which is part of the body's hormonal system). Inside the brain are fluid-filled **ventricles**.

▽ The brain is a hollow organ. Inside are the ventricles, a linked set of cavities and tunnels which extend down into the spinal cord. They contain cerebrospinal fluid, which circulates slowly around the system, helping to nourish the brain tissue and carry away some waste materials.

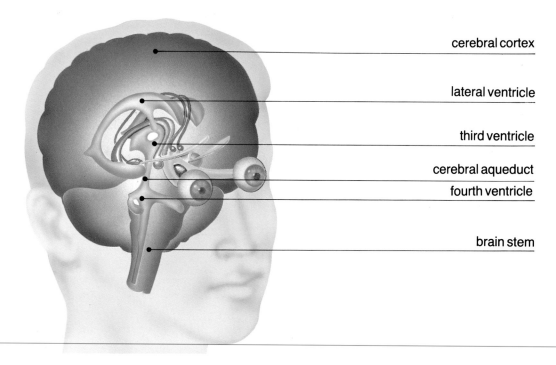

cerebral cortex

lateral ventricle

third ventricle

cerebral aqueduct
fourth ventricle

brain stem

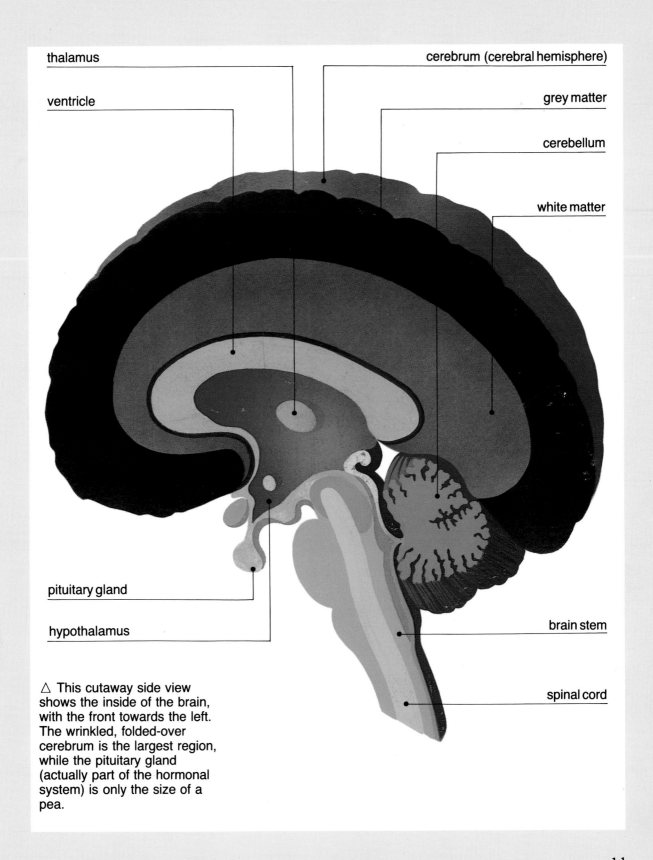

thalamus

ventricle

cerebrum (cerebral hemisphere)

grey matter

cerebellum

white matter

pituitary gland

hypothalamus

brain stem

spinal cord

△ This cutaway side view shows the inside of the brain, with the front towards the left. The wrinkled, folded-over cerebrum is the largest region, while the pituitary gland (actually part of the hormonal system) is only the size of a pea.

The "primitive" brain

The study of other animals, and the way they have evolved in the past (as shown by fossils), tell us much about the human body. The brain stem is sometimes called the "oldest" or most "primitive" region of the brain. This is because evolutionary studies show that, in complex animals, the brain stem was one of the first parts of the brain to develop. In fact, some scientists call it the "reptilian brain" since this region seems to have evolved first in the reptile group, and birds and mammals (including humans) are descended from reptiles.

The human brain stem is involved in control of the most basic body functions, such as heartbeat,

▽ A cutaway view of the brain from the side shows the brain stem in red (left). A view from the front reveals how nerves cross over in the brain stem, so that the left side of the brain controls the right side of the body, and vice versa.

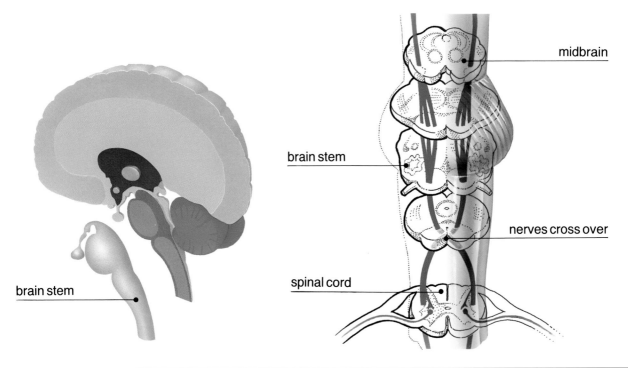

brain stem

midbrain

brain stem

nerves cross over

spinal cord

blood pressure, digestion and breathing.

Many of the activities involving the brain stem happen automatically. You do not have to remember to breathe or to make your heart beat. Nerves run from the chest muscles and heart, up the spinal cord to the brain stem, and back down again. At rest, breathing and heartbeat happen slowly. During exercise, the brain stem instructs the lungs to breathe more deeply and the heart to speed up, in order to supply the body's muscles with the extra oxygen they need. Messages pass to and fro between the brain stem, autonomic nerves (page 32), heart and chest muscles – but they do not reach the "higher" regions of the brain, where we would become aware of them.

Above the brain stem is the hypothalamus, a region of nerve cells about as big as the end of your thumb. It has one of the richest blood supplies in the whole body. Between them, the hypothalamus and brain stem take part in feelings such as hunger and thirst, anger and pleasure, and sexual arousal. They also help to keep body temperature constant, at about 36-37°C.

In the centre of the brain stem is a region of densely-packed nerve cells known as the **reticular formation**. This is the "watchguard" of the brain. Every second, millions of nerve messages arrive at the brain via the spinal cord, from the rest of the body. The reticular formation is thought to assess and filter the messages, letting through only a few important ones to the cerebrum above. In this way, you are aware of only a few important things at any one time. Otherwise the brain would be swamped by messages – most of them unimportant. As one scientist said: "With so much of interest happening around us, we can't afford to notice the way our socks feel on our feet."

Brain death

- In the past, death was thought to happen when the heart stopped or breathing ceased.
- Modern medical techniques can now restart the heartbeat or breathing. In some cases, people have recovered even after they have had no heartbeat or breathing for several minutes.
- In recent years, therefore, doctors have taken into account brain activity in the definition of "death".
- The brain stem controls basic functions such as breathing and heartbeat. So it is possible for the body to remain alive even after most of the rest of the brain has been destroyed – although the person would not regain consciousness.
- But if the brain stem is also destroyed, by injury or disease, there is no possibility of recovery.

Balance and co-ordination

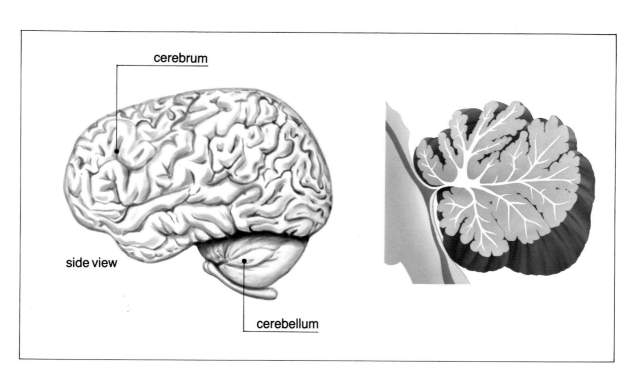

cerebrum

side view

cerebellum

The cerebellum, below and to the rear of the brain, is only about one-eighth the size of the cerebrum. Unlike the spinal cord and most of the brain stem, which have grey matter on the inside and white matter outside, the cerebellum has white matter as its core, covered by a layer of grey matter.

The arrangement of nerve cells inside the cerebellum is different from the rest of the brain. The cells are positioned with almost mathematical precision, in a complicated but regular way, like the wiring diagram for a computer. This region's main function is to process nerve messages concerning muscular movements from the cerebrum.

△ In a side view of the brain, the cerebellum is partly covered by the larger cerebrum (above left). A cutaway view shows that the cerebellum is, in effect, an outgrowth from the brain stem, with deep folds and creases (above right). It contains more nerve cells than the cerebrum.

▷ Even upside down and under water, the synchronized swimmer's cerebellum is filtering and refining nerve messages to make movements smooth and well balanced.

The "young" brain

The cerebrum is probably the "youngest" part of the brain – that is, the region which evolved most recently. In humans, compared to nearly all other animals, the cerebrum is enormous in proportion to the rest of the brain. It makes up about seven-tenths of the entire brain volume. The cerebrum is involved in processes such as thinking, reasoning, learning and memory – the basic aspects of what we call "intelligence".

The cerebrum is composed of two large domes, the cerebral hemispheres, separated by a deep groove along the middle called the cerebral fissure. The two **hemispheres** are joined by a "bridge" of brain tissue, the **corpus callosum**.

Like the cerebellum, the cerebrum has grey

▽ The cerebral hemispheres have a characteristic pattern of ridges, called gyri, and grooves known as sulci, each with its own name. (Some examples are shown below left.) Inside each hemisphere is white matter, which consists mainly of the long wire-like extensions of nerve cells, and also the fluid-filled ventricles (below right).

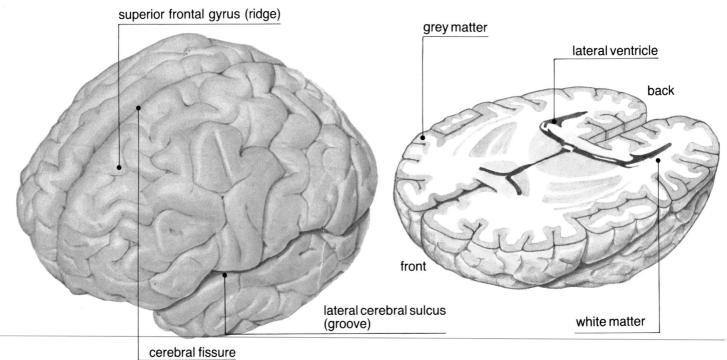

superior frontal gyrus (ridge)

grey matter

lateral ventricle

back

front

lateral cerebral sulcus (groove)

cerebral fissure

white matter

matter (composed mainly of the bodies of nerve cells) on the outside. This forms a layer known as the cerebral **cortex**, often simply called "the cortex". Under the cortex lies the white matter.

The cortex varies in thickness from about 2 to 4 millimetres. It is also deeply folded and creased. This means it has a much larger surface area than if it were smooth – and a large surface area means more nerve cells can be packed in. If the cortex was flattened out, it would have about the same area as a pillowcase. The cortex's folded structure, allowing extra nerve cells, may be one of the reasons why the human brain is capable of intelligent thought, compared to other animals in which the cortex is smoother.

△ Learning and memory are at their peak during the early years of life. A child takes in and remembers enormous amounts of information – not only the meaning of the words on the page, but what they look like and the colours of the pictures.

The nerve cells: neurons

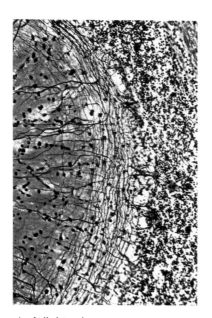

△ A light microscope photograph of nerve cells from the cerebellum. The dark spots are cell bodies. Some of the larger axons and dendrites show up as thin strands, but many others are too small to see.

The microscopic nerve cells that make up the brain, spinal cord and peripheral nerves are called neurons. There are probably 10,000 million neurons in the cortex alone, perhaps 100,000 million in the entire brain, and millions more in the spinal cord and peripheral nerves.

The brain is made not only of neurons. Packed tightly around and between the neurons are **neuroglial** ("nerve glue") **cells**, which make up about half the volume of the brain. They provide a supporting framework, like scaffolding, for the neurons. Some kinds of neuroglial cells also take part in nerve activity. In addition, like other body organs, the brain, spinal cord and nerves contain vessels which supply nourishing blood.

A typical neuron has three main parts. One is the "body", which is similar to other types of cell. It contains the nucleus (cellular control centre) and other structures commonly found in cells. The second part of the neuron consists of short, branching extensions from the cell body, called **dendrites**. The third part is a long, thin extension from the cell body, known as the axon. This is so thin that it can only be seen under a microscope, but in some neurons it is extremely long. Neurons in the nerves that link the feet to the spinal cord may have axons more than one metre long. In some types of neurons, the axon is enclosed in a sheath of fatty material called myelin, much as an electrical wire is surrounded by a plastic insulating cover.

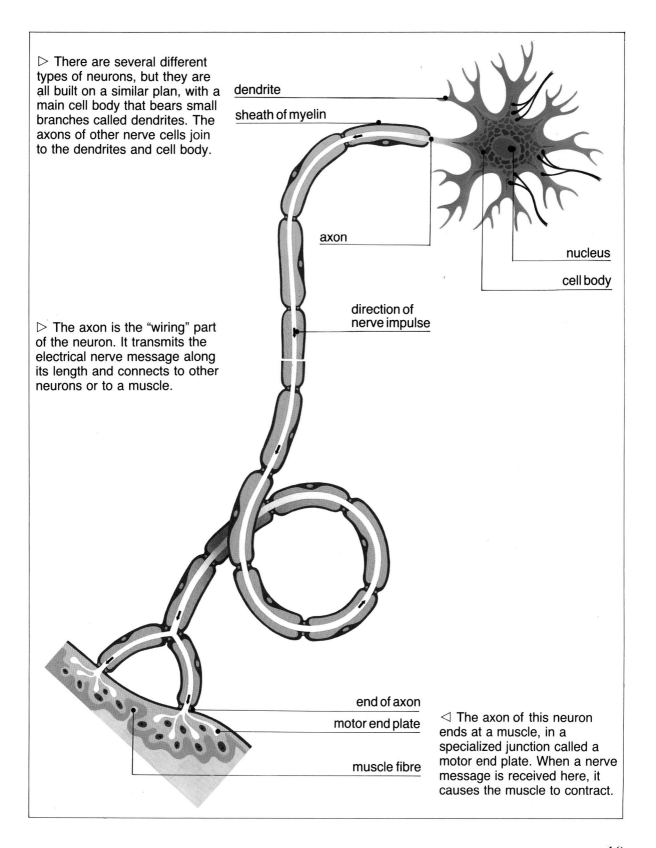

▷ There are several different types of neurons, but they are all built on a similar plan, with a main cell body that bears small branches called dendrites. The axons of other nerve cells join to the dendrites and cell body.

dendrite

sheath of myelin

axon

nucleus

cell body

direction of nerve impulse

▷ The axon is the "wiring" part of the neuron. It transmits the electrical nerve message along its length and connects to other neurons or to a muscle.

end of axon

motor end plate

muscle fibre

◁ The axon of this neuron ends at a muscle, in a specialized junction called a motor end plate. When a nerve message is received here, it causes the muscle to contract.

19

The neuron network

The billions of neurons in the nervous system pass on nerve messages, which are in the form of tiny bursts of electricity. But nerve messages do not simply pass from one neuron to the next. The dendrites and the axon endings branch to touch many other neurons, so that one neuron is in contact with numerous neighbours. The number of interconnections in the entire nervous system is staggering. The different paths that an individual nerve message could take is almost never-ending.

Also, not all neurons work in the same way. Some are excitatory, and pass on their nerve messages to excite, or stimulate, other neurons farther along the pathway. Others are inhibitory, and when they pass on their messages they inhibit, or damp down, the response of the receiving neurons.

It is probable that our thoughts, feelings and memories exist as particular patterns of nerve messages, passing repeatedly along certain pathways in the brain. Each message would "burn" a specific pathway among the billions of axons and dendrites.

Neurons, unlike other cells such as those in the blood or skin, cannot grow again, or repair themselves, or multiply to form new neurons. When you are born, you have virtually all the neurons you will ever have. Even before birth, brain neurons start to die off at the rate of thousands each day. However, there are so many neurons that usually this loss is not noticeable.

How many connections?

- An average neuron is connected to at least 50,000 others, and some are linked to five times as many.
- In one study, scientists estimated that a column of cortex only 1 mm square and 2.5 mm deep contained over 60,000 neurons.
- In this tiny fragment of brain tissue there could be more than 10,000 million interconnections between neurons.
- It is almost impossible to calculate the number of interconnections in the entire brain, with its 100,000 million neurons.

The brain can select different sets of pathways to get similar results. Because of this feature, people can generally cope with the loss of many thousands of neurons as they become older. Some people can overcome brain injury or disease, when whole regions of the brain are destroyed, by "learning" again using different parts of the brain.

For example, in a **stroke**, an artery supplying blood to a region of the brain may become blocked for some reason. The region of the brain supplied by that artery is starved of blood and may well die. The person may then not be able to carry out activities which relied on that region, such as limb movements or speech. However, given time, it is possible for some people who have had a stroke to "re-learn" such activities.

△ This scanning electron microscope photograph shows a tangle of nerve bodies, axons and dendrites from the brain's cortex. The long, thin axons are the "wires" of the nervous system. They carry nerve messages in the form of tiny bursts of electrical signals, like pulses of electricity passing along the cables inside a computer.

Ions and synapses

A nerve message passing along a neuron might seem like an electrical current travelling steadily along a wire, but in reality it is not the same. The axon is a thin tube filled with chemicals dissolved in water. Nerve messages travel in rapid bursts and rely on the movement of **ions**, which are tiny electrically-charged particles.

The two main types of ions involved are those of potassium and sodium, two common metallic substances. Normally there is more potassium inside the axon and more sodium in the fluid surrounding it. The inside of the axon has a

▽ At the synapse, nerve messages are carried across the tiny gap by **neurotransmitter chemicals**. When the message reaches the end of the axon, tiny "bubbles" or vesicles release the chemicals. These travel across the gap, and stimulate the surface membrane of the next neuron to re-create the nerve message. The gap in a typical synapse is only 25 nanometres (0.000025 mm) across.

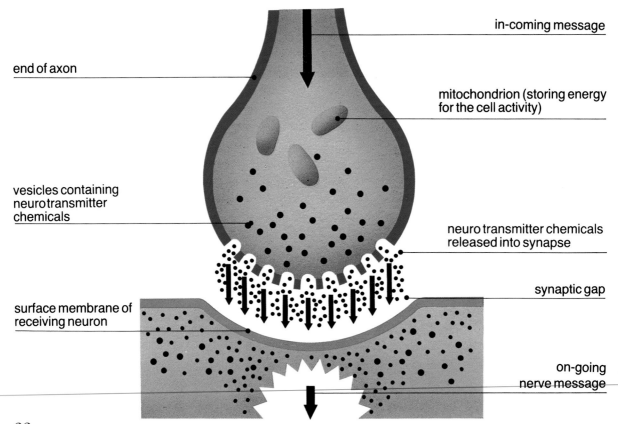

in-coming message

end of axon

mitochondrion (storing energy for the cell activity)

vesicles containing neurotransmitter chemicals

neuro transmitter chemicals released into synapse

synaptic gap

surface membrane of receiving neuron

on-going nerve message

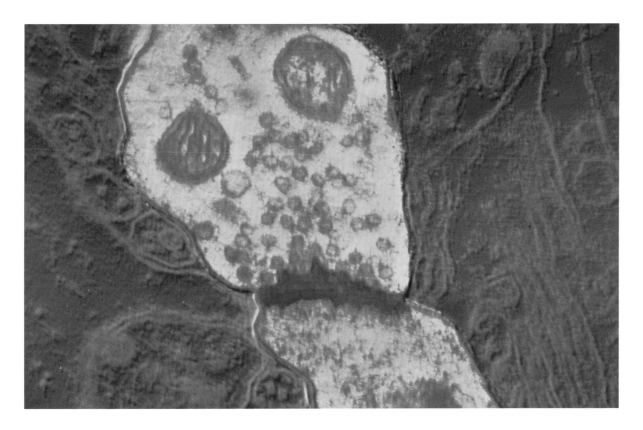

slightly negative charge and the outside has a positive charge. As a nerve message arrives, the axon's membrane (its thin "skin") changes to allow ions to leak through. Sodium ions flow in, while some potassium ions pass out. This causes a sudden alteration in the electrical balance at that point, the inside of the membrane becoming positive instead of negative.

As the message passes onwards, the ions move back to restore the resting balance. This state of ionic exchange surges along the axon like a wave, representing the travelling message. The whole process happens in one-thousandth of a second.

Neurons do not actually touch each other. There are tiny gaps between them, called **synapses**. Here the nerve message "jumps" across the gap by means of special chemicals known as neurotransmitters.

△ Under the transmission electron microscope, the actual junction between two nerves can be seen. The junction, or synapse, shows up deep red in the centre. Just above the junction are small bubble-like vesicles of neurotransmitter chemical. The two larger objects near the top are mitochondria, the cell's energy producers. (This view is magnified almost 100,000 times, and the colours have been added by computer to make the picture clearer.)

Brain waves

All the time, even when you are asleep, millions of tiny electrical messages are passing to and fro inside the brain and over its surface. Although they are very small, these signals can be detected and measured by a device known as an electro-encephalograph. This is because body tissues are good conductors of electricity. The signals pass out from the brain, through the muscles and skin, like ripples on the water's surface. The metal sensors of the electro-encephalograph are attached to the skin of the head and detect the signals.

The signals are amplified within the device, and displayed as a wavy trace on a television monitor screen or paper chart. This display is called an electro-encephalogram, or **EEG**.

▽ Having an EEG is painless and can even be good fun!

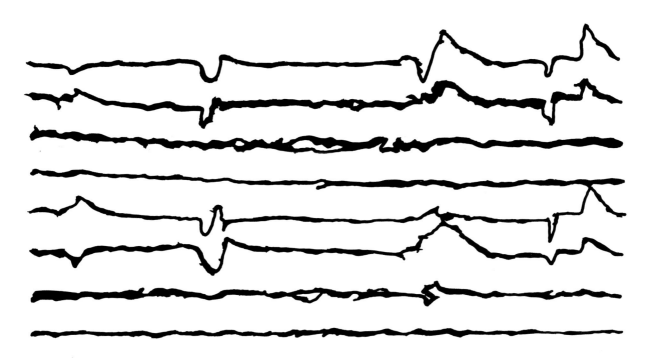

△ The jagged lines of the EEG "brain waves" recording.

EEGs and X-ray scans, such as **CAT scans**, are useful because without them it is difficult to examine the brain itself, encased inside the skull. EEGs help in the diagnosis of certain illnesses, such as epilepsy and brain tumours.

An EEG shows that electrical signals are not produced steadily by the brain. Instead they come in regular short bursts. These produce a pattern on the EEG like a series of waves, sometimes called "brain waves". The shapes of the waves are characteristic of the brain's activity. When you are awake but relaxed, they are fast and small. This is called the alpha rhythm. Intense thought or moving around causes the sharper, more jagged waves of the beta rhythm. When you are deeply asleep, your brain produces large, slow waves known as the delta rhythm (page 26). The theta rhythm is seen in babies and during sleep.

Epilepsy

In the condition known as epilepsy, the brain's regular and organized electrical activity is suddenly disturbed. Neurons fire messages at random, and these may cause temporary loss of consciousness. Messages may also pass to the muscles to produce the unco-ordinated movements known as a convulsion (also called a fit or seizure).

There are various types of epilepsy, diagnosed by the nature of the convulsion (if present) and the shape of the EEG recording. About 1 person in 200 has epilepsy. In most cases, it can be controlled by anti-convulsant drugs.

25

The sleeping brain

Most of us spend about a third of our lives asleep. What do the brain and body do at this time? Scientists have studied sleep using various techniques, such as EEGs, skin electrical-resistance sensors and muscle-activity detectors.

As you fall asleep, you drift in and out of consciousness. You may feel as if you are floating. This is known as stage 1 sleep. Heartbeat and breathing slow down, muscles relax, and a slight noise would wake you. After a few minutes, you pass to stage 2. The EEG trace shows "sleep spindles", the eyes roll slowly beneath closed lids, and louder noises are needed to wake you.

Stage 3 involves the appearance on the EEG of the long, slow waves of the delta rhythm.

How much sleep?

The amount of sleep we need varies enormously between different people. However, on average:
- babies sleep for about 16 hours each day, in several periods;
- at five years of age, most children sleep for 10-11 hours each night;
- adults tend to need about 7-8 hours' sleep each night, to stay healthy and alert.
- Illness, great exertion and pregnancy all increase the need for sleep.
- A few people are "nonsomniacs" and need only 1-2 hours' sleep nightly.

◁ At the end of the story *Alice In Wonderland*, Alice is showered with playing-card people from her dream. Then she wakes – and the cards are really dead leaves, drifting onto her face from the tree above. Alice had put the real leaves into her dream.

Heartbeat, breathing and blood pressure fall further, as does body temperature, and muscles become more relaxed.

About 20 to 30 minutes after falling asleep, you enter stage 4. The EEG shows mainly delta waves, and you are now deeply asleep. You might talk in your sleep, or even sleep-walk.

Over the next 30 to 40 minutes this pattern is reversed. But back at stage 1, the eyes suddenly start to flicker to and fro, while breathing and heartbeat become irregular. This is known as **REM (Rapid Eye Movement) sleep**. Woken at this time, you might say that you had been in the middle of a dream.

Periods of REM sleep then alternate with NREM (non-REM) sleep, in about a 90-minute cycle. The REM portion becomes longer each time, while the non-REM one shortens. The fourth or fifth period of REM sleep might last one hour. Finally, sleep becomes shallower – and you are awake.

▽ This lady drowsing in the "sleep laboratory" has electrodes (metal sensors) stuck to her head, connected to an EEG machine. Several research centres carry out investigations into what happens when we are asleep. But the reason why we sleep is still not clear. It may be a time when the brain processes the masses of information it has received during the day, discarding some and "filing" others in the memory.

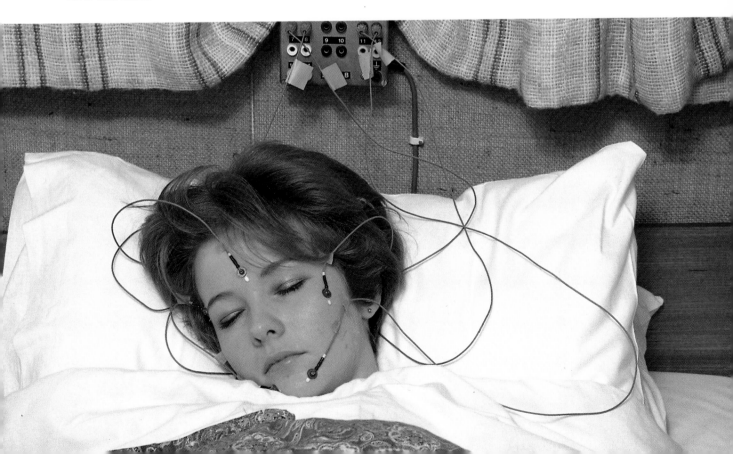

Between brain and body

Nerve messages, flashing to and fro among the network of neurons, do not stay in the brain. Throughout the body, the sensory nerves carry information to the brain, while motor nerves transmit messages from the brain to the muscles.

A typical "nerve" is a bundle of axons, perhaps hundreds or thousands, plus a few scattered neuron bodies. Neuron bodies are clumped more densely in small lumps, called **ganglia**.

The neurons vary in size and shape. Some of the large motor neurons in the spinal cord have cell bodies about 0.1 millimetres across, compared to certain neurons in the cerebral cortex, which have cell bodies only 0.005 millimetres across. Similarly, axons vary in diameter from 0.5 to 20 micrometres (0.0005 to 0.02 millimetres).

Not all nerve messages travel at the same speed. For example, you may have noticed that when you stub your toe, you are aware of touch and light pressure on the toe within a fraction of a second – but you do not feel the aching pain until slightly later. This is because the sensory nerves carrying messages about touch and pressure on the skin work quite fast, whereas the nerves transmitting messages about tissue damage and pain work more slowly. In an adult, the distance between the toe and brain is often more than one and a half metres. This makes the time difference between the arrival of touch messages and pain messages in the brain quite noticeable, at more than one second.

The speed of the message

- The speed at which a nerve message travels depends on various features, such as the thickness of the axon and whether it is coated with a fatty sheath of myelin.
- Thick axons and **myelin sheaths** both increase the speed of conduction.
- A "fast" nerve can conduct the message at more than 120 m per second.
- A "slow" nerve transmits the message at 0.5 m per second.
- These speeds are slow compared to the speed of electricity in a wire, which is nearly 300,000,000 m per second!

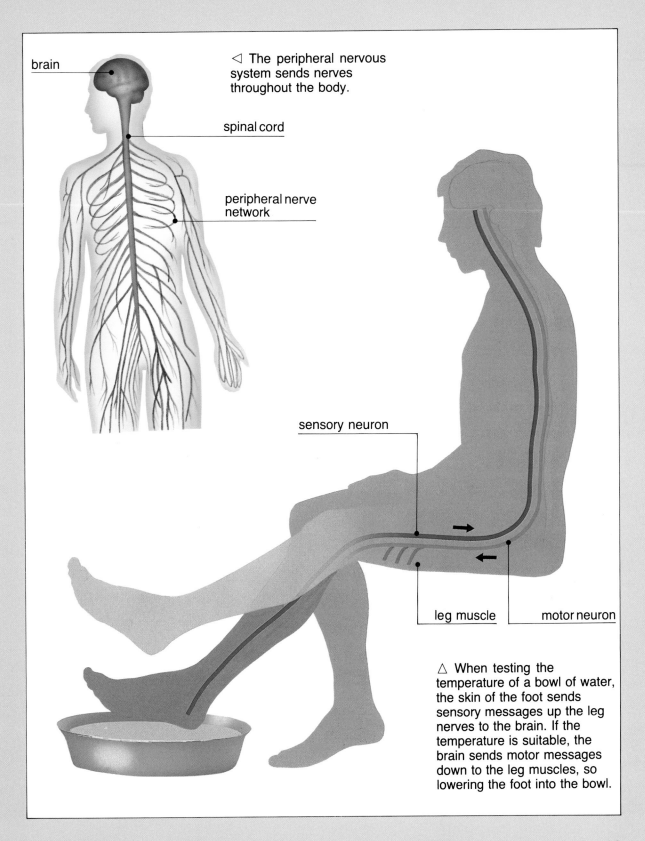

brain

◁ The peripheral nervous system sends nerves throughout the body.

spinal cord

peripheral nerve network

sensory neuron

leg muscle

motor neuron

△ When testing the temperature of a bowl of water, the skin of the foot sends sensory messages up the leg nerves to the brain. If the temperature is suitable, the brain sends motor messages down to the leg muscles, so lowering the foot into the bowl.

29

Reflex actions

Control by the brain is essential for many of our actions. But sometimes it is necessary for the body to react as quickly as possible, without waiting for the brain (which may be busy elsewhere) to take notice and give instructions. These emergency reactions are called **reflexes**.

Many reflexes involve making a sudden movement in response to the threat of physical damage, such as a pin-prick or the heat of a flame. For example, if you put your hand too near a hot saucepan and feel the heat coming off, you jerk your hand away almost before you have realized the danger. If something comes too close to your eyes, you automatically close their lids, and perhaps throw up your hands too.

Most reflexes work in the same basic way. If you prick your finger on a pin, sensors in the skin flash warning messages along the nerves, up the

▽ This cross-section through the spinal cord shows how sensory nerve messages enter the spinal cord, travel around the reflex loop, and pass straight out again to the muscles – without involving the brain.

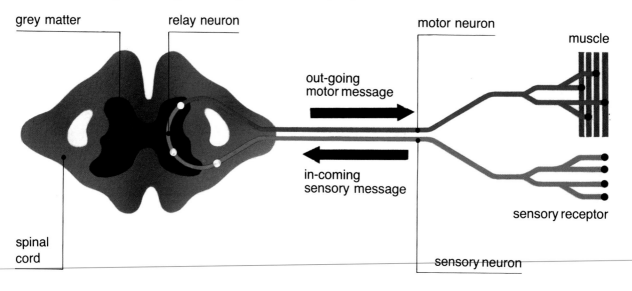

grey matter

relay neuron

motor neuron

muscle

out-going
motor message

in-coming
sensory message

sensory receptor

spinal
cord

sensory neuron

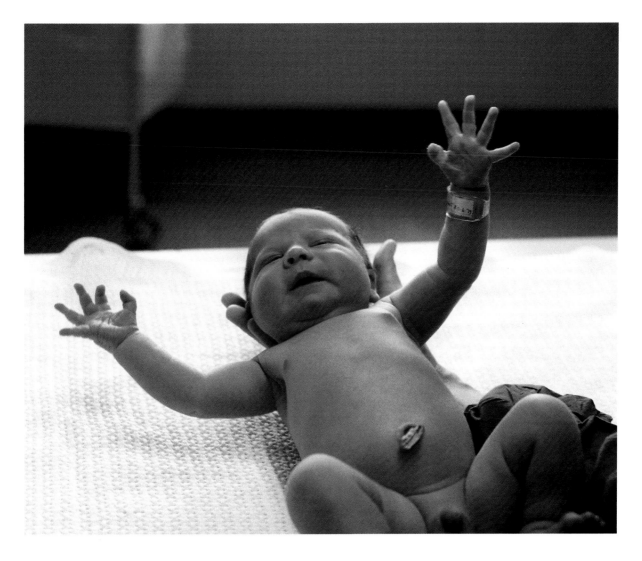

hand and arm, to the spinal cord. The messages are conveyed to neurons in the central grey matter of the cord. Here, they split up and follow two paths. One path follows a short reflex loop through the spinal cord, via relay neurons, and back out along motor neurons, down to the muscles of the arm and hand. Almost at once, the muscles contract to pull your finger away.

Some messages follow the second path, up the spinal cord to the brain. When they arrive, you become aware of the pin-prick, but the reflex loop has already caused your finger to be pulled away.

△ New babies have many reflexes, but they learn to control many of them as they grow older. In the Moro or "startle" reflex, if a baby is allowed to fall backwards a little way, he or she throws out arms and legs and clutches with the fingers.

Running on automatic

We are very much aware of some activities of the nervous system, such as thinking hard, or controlling complicated movements as when drawing a picture. But the nervous system is also working without us realizing it. Every minute the heart beats, the lungs breathe, the intestines push food through, the glands release their products, and many other activities happen in the body. All these internal activities need to be controlled.

The internal monitoring and control of body organs is carried out by a special part of the nervous system, known as the **autonomic nervous system**. It regulates blood circulation, breathing, digestion, elimination of wastes from the body, and the reproductive organs. It works "automatically", so that we do not have to think about its functions. And it operates in harmony with the hormonal system, in which glands release substances called hormones into the bloodstream. The hormones affect other organs, making them work faster or slower as necessary.

The autonomic nervous system works independently of most of the brain. Many of its neurons are grouped in ganglia near the spine, and it has its own nerves running to the major organs. It operates mainly by reflexes, and the brain stem is also involved in its activity (page 12). We are rarely conscious of its functions.

This nervous system is split into two parts, termed the **sympathetic** and **parasympathetic nervous systems**. They work against each other

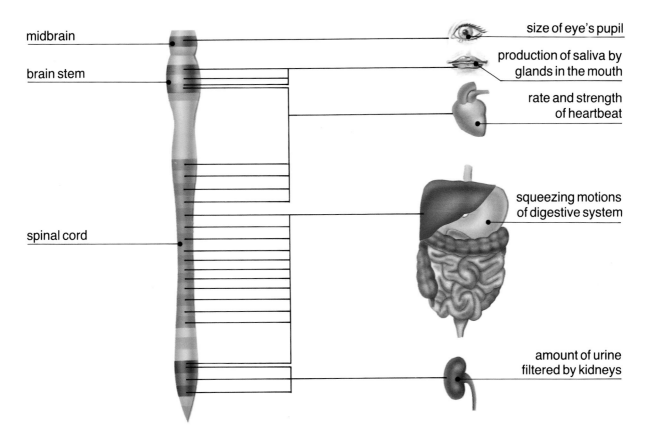

midbrain

brain stem

spinal cord

size of eye's pupil

production of saliva by glands in the mouth

rate and strength of heartbeat

squeezing motions of digestive system

amount of urine filtered by kidneys

in a "push-pull" fashion. One system stimulates a particular organ to work harder, while the other inhibits it and makes it slow down. The balance between the two systems keeps the internal organs working at the correct rate for the circumstances – whether resting in a chair or running for a bus.

Most of our everyday body functions are controlled largely by the parasympathetic nervous system. When we become angry or frightened, the sympathetic nervous system takes over. Working with the hormonal system it makes the heart beat faster, the lungs breathe more deeply, the pupils of the eyes widen, and it diverts blood flow to the muscles at the expense of the skin and intestines. The result: we turn pale and get ready for action, become extra-aware and prepared for any emergency. This is called the "fight or flight" reaction.

△ Nerves of the autonomic system run from the brain and spinal cord, to control various "automatic" movements of the body. For example, the eye's pupil constantly changes size according to the amount of light coming into the eye; while the digestive system automatically squirms and squeezes foods along its length, day and night.

The map of the cortex

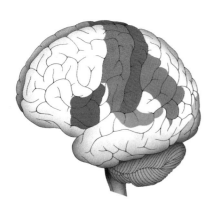

△ Areas of the cortex: motor (pink), touch (blue), vision (yellow), speech production (red) and hearing (orange).

The muscles of our internal organs work largely automatically, controlled by the autonomic nervous system. But many of the muscles that move our head, body and limbs work only when we want them to. They are called voluntary muscles, and they are controlled directly by the cortex of the brain.

Across the cortex of each cerebral hemisphere is a narrow strip known as the **motor area**. This is concerned with initiating and organizing our movements. Its neurons collect information from other parts of the brain, including signals from sense organs. When a decision has been made to move a body part, the motor cortex sends out

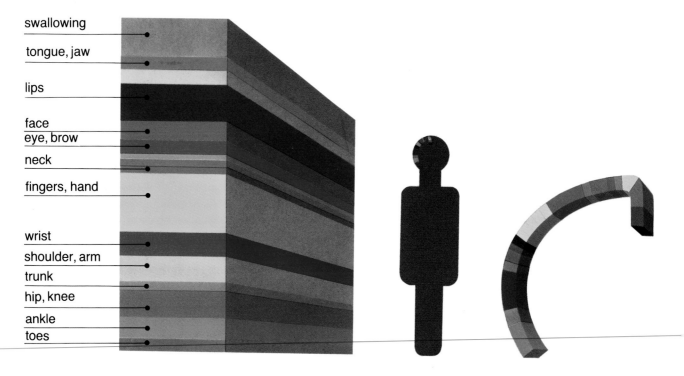

swallowing
tongue, jaw
lips
face
eye, brow
neck
fingers, hand
wrist
shoulder, arm
trunk
hip, knee
ankle
toes

nerve messages along motor nerves, to the muscles which pull on that part.

The messages may well pass through the cerebellum on their way to the muscles. Here they are further refined and co-ordinated, to make the movements smooth and well-balanced. Even a simple action, such as waving goodbye, requires the careful co-ordination of dozens of muscles, working together in various teams.

Different parts of the motor area have special functions, each controlling the muscles in a certain part of the body. Important and complex parts, such as the hands and mouth, require very fine control, and the many neurons needed for this work take up a relatively large portion of the motor area.

In the same way that movements are controlled by the motor area, so other areas of the cortex deal with sensory information coming in from the eyes, ears, nose, tongue and other sense organs.

▽ The relative portions of the cortex dealing with motor functions (below left) and the senses (below) are shown in diagrammatic form. Parts which need fine control and which are very sensitive, such as the fingers, take up correspondingly larger portions of the cortex.

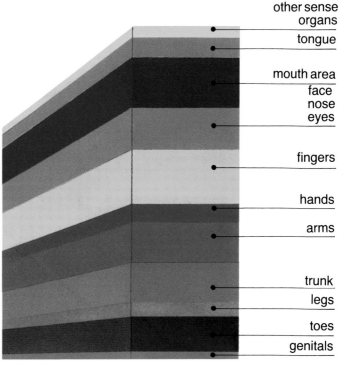

other sense organs
tongue
mouth area
face
nose
eyes
fingers
hands
arms
trunk
legs
toes
genitals

Reason and creation

The cerebral hemispheres are joined by a "bridge" of nerve tissue, the corpus callosum, at the base of the deep groove between them. In some brain operations, the two hemispheres have had to be completely separated (although each is still connected to parts of the brain below). And in some accidents, one or other hemisphere has been badly damaged. When this has happened, in many cases the behaviour of the person showed that each hemisphere could function on its own, as a separate "brain" – but the right and left sides worked in very different ways.

In most people, the left side of the brain takes the lead in "logical" thinking. This is the sort of careful, step-by-step reasoning that we use to solve a mathematical problem, for example, or

▽ A chess match between a human brain and an electronic one, in the shape of a computer. The left hemisphere takes the lead in this area of thought. A modern computer chess program can beat the average club player, but the chess game itself and the program both came from the human mind.

work out the next move in a chess game. The left side also predominates in speech, which is an immensely complex process involving choosing words, stringing them together into sentences, and instructing the throat and mouth to speak them.

In most people, the right side of the brain is the more "artistic" part. It tends to be more important for creative things, such as painting, music, solving visual puzzles and recognizing objects like a familiar face in a crowded room. The right side looks at situations and problems in general, and "jumps" to an immediate answer or solution. The left side deals with the more abstract symbols of language and also logic.

△ Creative activities tend to have their basis in the right hemisphere of the brain. This lady is crafting and finishing a violin, which in simplest terms is made from pieces of wood and pots of varnish. Such complex human actions are built up from experience and intuition. It is difficult to explain to an outsider exactly how they should be done.

The learning brain

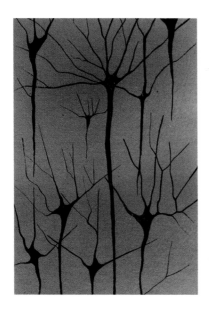

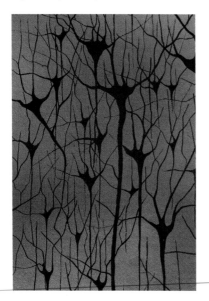

△ ▽ Connections between neurons increase markedly between 3 months (above) and 2 years (below).

As soon as a baby is born, it begins to learn. It soon recognizes faces, and realizes that if it cries for long enough, it will be fed or comforted. During the early years we learn to walk, talk, read and write and do many other amazing feats. It is estimated that half of our total life's learning happens within a year or two of starting school.

How do we "learn"? The process is believed to rely on new pathways being established among the vast network of neurons in the brain. For example, suppose you are learning to play the harp. Your brain sends out messages to the muscles in your arms and hands, to place your fingers in a particular position and then pluck the strings. The messages probably travel through existing pathways, and at first the movements are slow and unco-ordinated.

With more practice, the same messages are passed more often. The neural pathways begin to change, bringing together groups of messages and taking "short-cuts" through the maze of neurons. As new, faster, more co-ordinated pathways develop, you find that you can move your fingers more quickly and more precisely. Eventually you can play accurately and with feeling, without looking at your hands.

Studies have been carried out on the brains of children who have unfortunately died. New babies have fewer connections between their neurons, but the number increases rapidly as they quickly learn about the world around them.

Mathew age 3

Robert 5

Mark 7years

Thomas age 8

△ As children develop, so do their drawing skills. At first the human body is little more than a blob with hair. By eight years it has ears and teeth!

Memories are made of ...?

Types of memory

- Short-term memory lasts about a minute. We use it, for instance, to retain a phone number between reading it in the phone book and dialling.
- Short-term memory can hold only about 7 items (the length of many phone numbers).
- Long-term memory can last many decades.
- It is estimated that the human brain could hold more than 1,000 times the information contained in a large 20-volume encyclopedia.

Learning and many of our other mental abilities depend on memory. We do not only remember facts, such as the name of the world's highest mountain, which are mostly in the form of words. We remember patterns of movement, such as riding a bicycle or playing a harp. And we can recall sights, sounds, smells and tastes, and even the way we "felt" at an important event.

Memory consists of three stages. First is feeding the information we wish to remember into the brain; second is storing it there in some form; and third is retrieving it again for use.

Recent research has shown that at least two regions of the brain are central to memories. These are the hippocampus (from the Greek word

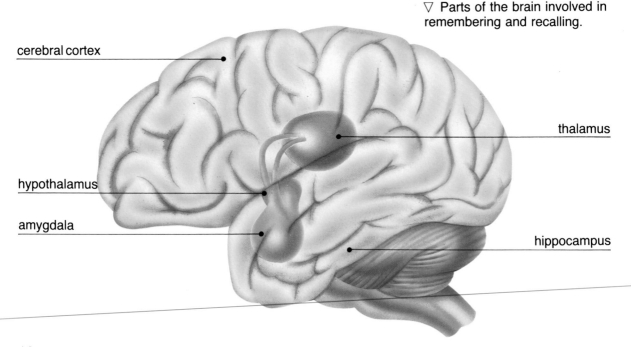

▽ Parts of the brain involved in remembering and recalling.

cerebral cortex

thalamus

hypothalamus

amygdala

hippocampus

for "sea horse", which it resembles in shape) and the amygdala (meaning "almond"). On each side of the brain, these regions are sandwiched between the brain stem to the inside and the inner folds of the cerebral hemispheres to the outside.

It is possible that information from the senses is first processed in the cerebral cortex. Next, we must wish to remember it, usually because it has some sort of importance in our lives. It is then passed inwards, in the form of nerve messages, to regions such as the hippocampus and amygdala. The messages then cycle around this pathway, affecting the way the neurons link together. So a "memory" may exist in the brain as a pattern of connections among the millions of neurons.

△ Many people recognize this scene from the 1988 Olympic Games in Seoul, South Korea. The Canadian sprinter Ben Johnson is just about to win the men's 100 metres final. But shortly after, he failed a drugs test and was disqualified. The brain can often recall events like these that happened in a sequence. For example, just mentioning the athlete's name would for many people trigger the memories of why he is well known, and when and where the race happened.

41

Mental health

It is relatively easy for most of us to recognize a physical illness. If we know someone has a heart disease, or a stroke, we can imagine the problems concerned and show understanding. But what about mental illness?

Most people are mentally healthy, most of the time. Their brain and nerves work well, and they think and behave fairly normally. They can cope with everyday living. Occasionally they may be affected by great stress, such as the death of a loved one, and become withdrawn or aggressive. But they recover gradually.

In mental illness, however, thoughts and behaviour become disturbed. This is usually because of problems in the brain and nervous system, and in the way the person reacts with other people and the outside world.

▷ The type of medical scan called PET (positron emission tomography) can be used to detect abnormally-working parts of the brain. This scan shows a horizontal "slice" of a normal, living brain, with computer-added colours to show levels of chemical activity. In a diseased brain, the colour pattern would show abnormal "hot spots" or "cold spots" of activity.

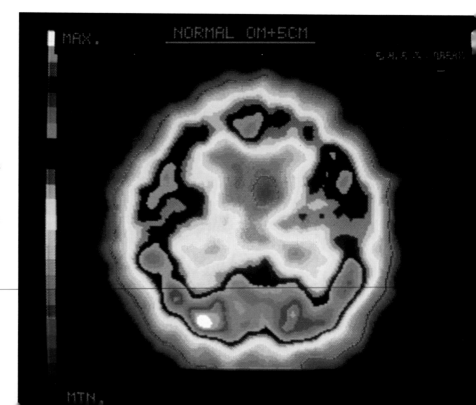

It may be difficult for us to understand this situation. For example, people who suffer from severe depression tend to remain sad and fed up, not take any interest in things, and say that life is hopeless. Because we all feel a little depressed now and again, we might urge them to "snap out of it" or "pull themselves together". This is like telling someone with arthritis to hurry up and cure themselves. Severe depression is a mental illness, and is as real as a physical illness such as arthritis. Depending on the severity of the illness, and how the person copes in everyday life, it may be wise to obtain the help of a psychiatrist, a doctor who specializes in mental problems.

Brain chemistry probably plays an important part in many mental illnesses. There may be a lack of certain neurotransmitters, or a certain region of the brain may not have developed properly in early life. Or parts of the brain could be damaged by infection, tumours or drugs. These sorts of causes affect the way the brain works, and so affect thought patterns and behaviour.

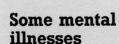

Some mental illnesses

- Depression is a deep misery, sadness and sense of hopelessness that cannot be shaken off. There may also be other symptoms such as loss of appetite and headaches.
- Schizophrenia is a "shattering" of thoughts and feelings, so that they become jumbled and vague. The person may hear imaginary voices, suddenly laugh or cry for no reason, or carry out strange movements. He or she lives in a fantasy world of jumbled judgements and behaviour.
- Phobias are unreasonable fears of objects or situations. Some people are afraid of spiders, but this does not generally interfere with everyday life. However a person with severe agoraphobia, for instance, may be terrified of open spaces and public places – so much so that he or she might not even be able to leave the house.
- Many mental illnesses can be treated, and even cured, with modern drugs and psychiatric techniques such as psychotherapy.

The wisdom of age

The brain and nervous system, like other parts of the body, eventually become less efficient with increasing age. We see this outwardly as a change in mental abilities and behaviour. Memories fade, reasoning becomes slower, and the ability to understand new ideas or processes tends to diminish. As this progresses the personality changes, there is confusion and disinterest and movements become more unco-ordinated. The condition begins to affect daily life and maybe independence. It is sometimes called "senility".

The rate at which this happens varies enormously. A few people show these signs in late middle age, while others remain alert and mentally fit at the age of 80 or beyond.

There is a gradual loss of neurons throughout life, in the brain, spinal cord and peripheral nerves. So we might expect some lessening of mental powers in old age. However, what may seem like "senility" is sometimes another problem, which can be helped. It may be loss of hearing, a mental illness, an infection, a stroke or lack of vitamins in food. With care and treatment, the symptoms may lessen.

However, a major problem faced by some old people is the attitude of others. Younger people may "expect" them to be mentally slow and incapable, and treat them as such. The old person may then decide to accept this and "give up". The old saying that "you are as fit as you feel" applies to the brain and mind as well as the body.

▷ A child can benefit from the experience and wisdom that age brings. And an older person can keep feeling alert and young-at-heart when in the stimulating company of a child. Young and old have much to learn from each other.

Glossary

Autonomic nervous system: the part of the nervous system that functions without our conscious awareness. It controls the life-support systems of the body.

Axon: long thread extending from the body of a neuron, along which a nerve message is carried.

Brain: main part of the central nervous system, housed in the skull, and the "control centre" of the whole body.

Brain stem: bulge at the top of the spinal cord, forming the bottom part of the brain. The brain stem controls most of our vital functions, and is a major part of the autonomic nervous system.

CAT scan: picture obtained by a computerized axial tomography scanner, in which a series of images are taken by very weak X-rays and processed by computer to show a "slice" through the body. It aids in diagnosis of disease.

Central nervous system: the brain and spinal cord are the most essential parts of the nervous system, together making up the central nervous system.

Cerebellum: small and deeply folded area at the back of the brain, concerned with controlling co-ordination of movement and balance.

Cerebral hemisphere: one half of the dome-shaped cerebrum; also simply called a hemisphere.

Cerebrospinal fluid: clear fluid that normally circulates through the ventricles of the brain and spinal cord and around the spaces between the meninges. It helps to cushion and nourish nerve tissues.

Cerebrum: large domed area making up the largest part of the brain. Our reasoning, memory and senses are controlled in the cerebrum.

Corpus callosum: small strip of tissue connecting the two hemispheres of the cerebrum. Signals passed between the right and left hemispheres cross the corpus callosum.

Cortex: the outer layer of the cerebrum, made up from grey matter.

Dendrites: the finely branched endings of an axon which are in contact with another neuron at the synapse.

EEG: electro-encephalogram; a measurement of the electrical activity within the brain, recorded as a graph on a strip of moving paper or TV screen.

Ganglia: small groups of neurons, in which nerve signals are processed.

Grey matter: part of the nerve tissue in which the bodies of the neurons are situated. Mostly on the *outside* of the brain, and the *inside* of the spinal cord.

Hemispheres: the two dome-like structures that make up most of the cerebrum. Also called cerebral hemispheres.

Hypothalamus: small part of the brain which is concerned with regulating autonomic functions (such as changes in pulse rate, sweating, etc.), controlling sleep, and governing the action of the most important gland in the body, the pituitary.

Ion: an electrically charged particle. When common salt, or sodium chloride, is dissolved in water, it splits into two separate ions: sodium and chloride.

Membrane: thin covering of a cell or tissue. Neurons are covered by a very thin membrane, through which transmitter chemicals pass.

Meninges: skin-like coverings over the brain and part of the spinal cord. There are three layers: the dura mater, arachnoid and pia mater.

Meningitis: inflammation and swelling of the meninges, often caused by germs such as bacteria or viruses. In severe cases it can be fatal.

Motor area: part of the surface of the cerebrum in which instructions for muscle movement are processed.

Myelin sheath: fatty covering of a nerve cells's axon, which helps to speed the passage of the nerve message and also isolate it electrically from neighbouring axons.

Nerve: bundle of axons, through which signals are passed to and from the brain.

Neuroglial cells: special cells

that are packed around and between the neurons. They help support the delicate nervous tissue.

Neuron: nerve cell that passes signals to other neurons along a thread-like axon.

Neurotransmitter chemicals: chemicals present in tiny amounts, which carry a signal across a synapse, between the neurons.

NMR scan: picture obtained by a nuclear magnetic resonance scanner (also called nuclear imaging), showing the structure and level of chemical activity in certain parts of the body. It aids in diagnosis of disease.

Parasympathetic nervous system: part of the autonomic nervous system which influences the pupil of the eye, pulse rate, breathing, digestion and sexual organs. Its action is, in general, opposite to that of the sympathetic nervous system.

Peripheral nervous system: network of nerves that run between the brain and spinal cord (the central nervous system), and the various sense organs and muscles throughout the body.

REM sleep: rapid eye movement sleep, a stage during which the eyes flicker to and fro under closed lids, and dreams are thought to occur.

Receptors: sensors, or groups of cells that can receive a signal, and pass it on to the nervous system. Typical receptors are those registering touch, in the skin, and light, in the retina of the eye.

Reflex: an automatic response of the body, which initially does not involve the brain. An example of a reflex is jerking the hand away from a hot object.

Reticular formation: central part of the brain that filters incoming nerve messages and passes important ones to the cerebrum.

Spinal cord: very large bundle of nerve cells running down from the brain inside the spine.

Stroke: death of part of the brain, with disruption of the senses or actions controlled by that part (such as touch or speech).

Sympathetic nervous system: part of the autonomic nervous system influencing pulse rate, breathing, and many other functions. Its actions are generally opposite to those of the parasympathetic nervous system, preparing the body for action in an emergency. It also controls speech and swallowing.

Synapse: the gap between a neuron and the dendrites of another neuron.

Thalamus: part of the brain that processes information from the sense organs, and provides some control over muscle activity.

Ventricles: fluid-filled spaces inside the brain, also running down the middle of the spinal cord.

White matter: masses of closely packed axons. White matter makes up most of the interior of the brain, and the outside of the spinal cord.

Index